THE EPISTLE TO THE GALATIANS

C. I. Scofield

*Addresses delivered at Sea Cliff Bible Conference,
July, 1903*

Grace Gospel Press
Duluth, Minnesota

The Epistle to the Galatians
by C. I. Scofield

Reprinted 2014 by Grace Gospel Press

ISBN 978-1-939110-05-3

GGP
Grace Gospel Press
201 W. Saint Andrews St.
Duluth, MN 55803
U.S.A.
(218) 724-5914
www.gracegospelpress.com

Printed in the United States of America

CONTENTS

The Epistle to the Galatians

1. First Address (1:1-2:14). 5

2. Second Address (2:15-3:24) 13

3. Third Address (3:25-5:24) 25

4. Fourth Address (3:25-5:24) 33

5. Fifth Address (5:25-6:18) 45

The Christian Doctrine of the Law 57

Chapter 1

FIRST ADDRESS
(1:1–2:14)

In entering upon the study of Galatians let us first of all remember the circumstances which called out the Epistle. Galatia, in the first century, was a province of Asia Minor. It was inhabited by a race of aliens to that part of the world: Gauls, not Greeks, not Syrians. Three centuries before Christ a torrent of barbarians poured into Greece, and amongst them were Gauls who, when the wave receded, remained in what came to be called Galatia. They had the Gallic characteristics, enthusiasm, affectionateness, and fickleness (Gal. 1:6; 3:1; 4:9, 10).

In Galatia, as elsewhere in his beloved Asia, Paul labored, with the usual result that churches were planted. But to Galatia, as elsewhere among Paul's converts, went Judaizing teachers, mingling with the pure meal of truth the evil leaven of legality. Let me be understood;

the law of God is neither evil nor leaven, but is holy, just and good. But the law is only good in use when that use is lawful: *"knowing this, that the law is not made for a righteous man, but for the lawless and disobedient, for the ungodly and sinners"* (1 Tim. 1:8-11). All this will appear more explicitly in a moment. For the present let it suffice to notice that it was this evil work of the Judaizers which called out the Epistle to the Galatians.

With this necessary preliminary word, let us pass next to the structure of the Epistle. It falls naturally into six sections or chief divisions, as follows:

Section I: The Apostolic Salutation (1:1-5).

Section II: The Theme of the Epistle (1:6-9).

Section III: The Vindication of Paul's Apostleship and the Divine Authority of Paul's Gospel (1:10-2:14).

Section IV: Justification Is by Faith without Law (2:15-3:24).

Section V: The Justified Sinner Is a Son, Not a Servant, and Is Neither under the Law as a Rule of Life, Nor as a Means of Sanctification (3:25-5:24).

Section VI: Exhortations and Conclusion (5:25-6:18).

First Address (1:1–2:14)

Having thus seen the divine order of this Book, let us now take up these divisions more at length.

Section I
The Apostolic Salutation (1:1-5)

Paul begins with the affirmation, so usual in his epistles, of the divine authority of his apostleship (v. 1). It was neither "of" man as to authority, nor even "by" man instrumentally—as by election, or lot, or ordination, but wholly by Jesus Christ and God the Father (Acts 22:6-15; 26:12-18). He joins with himself the brethren who are with him (v. 2), as being of like precious faith; and communicates to the Galatians not, as some say, the apostolic blessing (which is blessed foolishness), but the divine message of grace and peace from Father and Son—that Son whose sacrifice was meant to deliver the believer not only from sin, but also from this present evil age with all its religiosity and pretended law-keeping (vv. 3, 4).

Section II
The Theme of Galatians (1:6-9)

The Apostle had called the Galatians into the *grace* of Christ. Now "grace" means unmerited, unrecompensed favor. It is essential to get this clear. Add never so slight an admixture of law-works, as circumcision, or law effort, as of obedience to commandments, and "grace is no more grace." So absolutely is this true, that grace cannot even begin with us until the law has reduced us to speechless guilt (Rom. 3:19). So long as there is the slightest question of utter guilt, utter helplessness, there is no place for grace. If I am not, indeed, quite so good as I ought to be, but yet quite too good for Hell, I am not an object for the grace of God, but for the illuminating and convicting and death-dealing work of His law.

Grace is God's "kindness toward US" (Eph. 2:7) — us, "*who were dead in trespasses and sins*" (Eph. 2:1), "*aliens from the commonwealth of Israel, and strangers from the covenants of promise, having no hope, and without God in the world*" (Eph. 2:12). The law is "just" (Rom. 7:12), and therefore heartily approves goodness, and unsparingly condemns badness; but, save Jesus of Nazareth, the law never saw a naturally good man. Grace, on the contrary, is not looking for good men whom it may approve, for it is not grace, but mere justice, to approve goodness; but it is looking for condemned, guilty, speechless and helpless men whom it may save, sanctify and glorify.

Into grace, then, Paul had called the Galatians. What was his controversy with them? Just this: They were "removed" from the grace of Christ unto "another gospel" — though he is swift to add, "*which is not another*" (vv. 6, 7). There could not be another gospel. Change, modify,

First Address (1:1–2:14)

the grace of Christ by the smallest degree, and you no longer have a "gospel." A gospel is "glad tidings"; and the law is not glad tidings. "*What things soever the law saith, it saith to them who are under the law: that every mouth may be stopped, and all the world may become guilty before God*" (Rom. 3:19) — and surely that is no good news. The law, then, has but one language; it pronounces "all the world" — good, bad, and goody-good — *guilty*. The only way to escape is to get out of the "world," and the hand of grace alone opens that way of escape.

> *Remember that any so-called gospel which is not pure unadulterated grace is "another" gospel.*

But you say: What is a simple child of God, who knows no theology, to do? Just this: Remember that any so-called gospel which is not pure unadulterated *grace* is "another" gospel. If it proposes, under whatever specious guise, to win the favor of God by works, or goodness, or "character," or anything else which man can do, it is spurious. That is the unfailing test. But it is more than spurious; it is *accursed* – or rather the preachers of it are (vv. 8, 9). It is not I who says that, but the Spirit of God who says it by His apostle. This is unspeakably solemn. Not the *denial* of the Gospel even, is so awfully serious as to *pervert* the Gospel. Oh, that God may give His people in this day power to discriminate, to distinguish things which differ. Alas, it is discernment which seems so painfully wanting.

If a preacher is cultured, gentle, earnest, intellectual and broadly tolerant, the sheep of God run after him. He, of course, speaks beautifully about Christ, and uses the old words—redemption, the cross, even sacrifice and atonement—but what is his *gospel*? That is the crucial question. Is salvation perfect, entire, eternal, the alone work of Christ and the free gift of God to faith alone? Or does he say: "Character is salvation," even though he may add that Christ "helps" to form that character?

Section III
The Vindication of Paul's Apostleship and the Divine Authority of Paul's Gospel
(1:10 to 2:14)

To the Apostle Paul was committed that body of revelation which explains grace and defines the doctrine of the Church. Our Lord, indeed, predicted the Church (Matt. 16:18), but He did not describe it. Apart from the revelation through Paul, we should know almost nothing of the Church. To Paul also was committed that body of truth concerning salvation which forms what he calls "my gospel" and which is the great doctrinal basis of Christianity. It is, therefore, of the utmost importance, that Paul shall remind the Galatians who are forsaking him for teachers who claim a superior authority as coming from

First Address (1:1–2:14)

Jerusalem, and as pretending to speak for Peter or James, that they are turning not from a man, but from *God's* man.

Let us note briefly the steps of this demonstration: *First* of all, the Apostle appeals to the knowledge which the Galatian saints had of his character (1:10). He was no men-pleaser; but, on the contrary, sacrificed popularity to the cause of truth. He was therefore worthy of credence.

Second, he plainly asserts the divine origin of his gospel (1:11, 12). He received it, not by tradition, nor from man, but by revelation.

Third, as to the pretensions of the Judaizers, who made much of their affiliation with the church at Jerusalem, if any living man knew Judaism it was himself (1:13, 14). He had been a foremost Jew. Indeed, he was saved, not from immorality, idolatry, or atheism, but from Judaism. If, therefore, he had not exalted Mosaism in his evangelistic labors in Galatia, it was because it was the mere chrysalis, the mere empty shell, out of which the Gospel had emerged.

Fourth, Paul recounts his life from his conversion to show that he was not an apostle-taught man, but a divinely sent, divinely equipped witness (1:15-24).

Fifth, as to circumcision and the law, the Apostle had tested that very issue in Jerusalem itself (2:1-5). Going thither by revelation, he had taken with him Titus, a Greek, whose presence was seized upon by false brethren as an occasion to bring up the question of circumcision;

and there, in the very mother church whose authority the Judaizers exalted, the circumcision of Gentile converts was not required. Why, then, should circumcision be insisted on in Galatia?

Sixth, Paul's apostleship was fully acknowledged by James, Peter, and John, the very foremost of those who were apostles before him (2:6-10).

Seventh, since the Judaizers were claiming some special authorization from Peter, it became necessary to point out that Peter was by no means infallible. At Antioch he had so dissembled for fear of Jewish opinion that Paul had to publicly rebuke him (2:11-14).

Here, then, were the solid bases of the apostolic authority of him who had called them into the grace of Christ, whose direct revelation from Christ they were forsaking to follow men who made much of tradition and of human authority. And this question of the source of Paul's teaching, permit me to remind you, is by no means an obsolete question of interest only in the first century. It is a burning question today, in the twentieth century. Men speak of "Pauline" theology, as if Paul were a mere theologian, the framer of a system of Christian doctrine—a system with which one may disagree, in whole or in part, and still be a good Christian. Against these, as against the objectors of the first century, the truth runs that Paul spoke, even as to the very words (1 Cor. 2:13), not as a system-maker, but as the mouth of God (John 17:18, 20).

Chapter 2

SECOND ADDRESS
(2:15–3:24)

We resume at this hour the study of Paul's great Epistle to the churches of Galatia. Passing from the triumphant vindication of his apostolic authority, Paul next refutes the first form of the Galatian heresy—the contention, namely, that a sinner is not justified by faith only, but must add law-works.

Section IV
Justification Is by Faith without Works of Law
(2:15 to 3:24)

The course of this demonstration is like the resistless march of an armed host. Nothing can stand before it. The flimsy quibblings of ancient and modern legalists are scattered like the chaff of the summer threshing floor. But this march is, like that of a well-ordered army, by definite stages. It is an invasion in which every vantage point is fortified and made a solid base for the next advance.

Friends, let us give our hearts to these things. We have, most of us, been reared and now live under the influence of Galatianism. Protestant theology, alas, is for the most part, thoroughly Galatianized, in that neither law nor grace are given their distinct and separated places, as in the counsels of God, but are mingled together in one incoherent system. The law is no longer, as in the divine intent, a ministration of death (2 Cor. 3:7), of cursing (Gal. 3:10), or conviction (Rom. 3:19), because we are taught that we must try to keep it, and that by Divine help we may. Nor, on the other hand, does grace bring us into freedom, for we are kept under the law (see Rom. 6:14).

The Apostle, then, *first* informs the Galatians that even the Jews, the men of privilege-who are not Gentiles "without Christ . . . aliens from the commonwealth of Israel, and strangers from the covenants of promise, having no hope, and without God in the world" (Eph. 2:12), but "who are Israelites; to whom pertaineth the adoption, and the glory, and the covenants, and the giving of the law, and the service of God, and the promises; whose are the fathers, and of whom as concerning the flesh Christ came" (Rom. 9:4, 5) — even the Jews have believed in Jesus Christ that they might be justified by the faith of Christ, and not by the works of the law (2:15, 16).

Second Address (2:15–3:24)

But death has freed the believer from the law (v. 19). Here is a great principle upon which I must ask you to pause for a moment. It is not only that the believer is as to the law, a dead man, but the far deeper thing is true that it was the law which killed him. He is dead to the law, not through suicide, but through execution. The law which he violated has condemned and executed him. The law, finding him red-handed, did not exhort him to try again, but summarily slew him. How this was is made clear in verse 20: "I am crucified with Christ." However unreal that may seem to the saint as a matter of *experience*, it is to God, who gave the law, an *eternal fact*; and the important matter is not what the believer "feels," but what God *says*. Doubtless the believer is called upon (Rom. 6:11) to "reckon" that to be true which God avers to be true; but the believer's reckoning has to do with his experience, not with his justification—and, whether or not he so reckons himself, the fact remains immutable that to God he is, as to the law, an executed criminal. Justice has been completely vindicated, and it is no longer possible even to bring an accusation against him (Rom. 8:33, 34).

It is not possible to know Gospel liberty nor Gospel holiness until this great fundamental truth is clearly, bravely grasped. One may be a Christian, and a worthy and useful man, and be still under bondage to the law; but one can never have deliverance from the dominion of sin, nor know the true blessedness and rest of the Gospel and remain under the law. Therefore, once more, note that it is *death* which has broken the connection between the believer and the law: "The law hath dominion over a man as long as he liveth" (Rom. 7:1). "But now we are delivered from the law, that being dead wherein we were held" (Rom. 7:6). Nothing can be clearer.

But I hasten to add that there is a mere carnal and fleshly way of looking at our deliverance from the law, which is most unscriptural, and, I am persuaded, most dishonoring to God. It consists in rejoicing in a supposed deliverance from the principle of divine authority over the life—a deliverance into mere self-will and lawlessness.

The true ground of rejoicing is quite other than this. The believer is set free from that which condemned him, and which, though perfectly "holy, just and good" in itself, only incited the flesh to acts of rebellion (Rom. 7:7-13). No, the believer's co-crucifixion with Christ was to the end that "henceforth he should not serve sin" (Rom. 6:6).

Accordingly, the Apostle moves to the *second* statement, in which, indeed, he slightly anticipates the truth concerning the principle of the believer's life, to which truth he devotes the fifth section of the Epistle. That truth is two-fold: (1) Though crucified with Christ he is alive again because Christ now lives in him;

Second Address (2:15–3:24)

and (2) the principle by which his new life is governed is the *by-faith,* instead of the *by-law* principle (2:20). This, as has just been said, is not strictly germane to the question of justification, but the Apostle states it, apparently, to meet instantly a charge of antinomianism—a calumny which legalists perpetually fling at those who, in realized deliverance from law, are seeking holiness through faith.

Remember the steps: The believer is justified by faith; is dead to the law; is alive again because Christ lives in him; and the principle of his present life is the by-faith principle. This opens an immense door of hope concerning daily deliverance from the power of sin, because "all things are possible to him that believeth."

> *Protestant theology, alas, is for the most part, thoroughly Galatianized, in that neither law nor grace are given their distinct and separated places, as in the counsels of God, but are mingled together in one incoherent system.*

Justification, it may be remarked in passing, *is that act of God whereby He declares righteous all who believe in Jesus.* It is something which takes place *in the mind of God, not in the nervous system or emotional nature of the believer.*

17

The *third* proposition (v. 21) opens the whole question of righteousness. Here is another great word. It is used in Scripture in three senses — one bad, two good. The bad sense is self, or legal righteousness. The pharisee who thanked God that he was not as other men; the Apostle Paul, in Philippians 3:4-6, had that kind of righteousness. Fortunately, not only for himself but for us, Paul's legal righteousness came to a test in the white light of the shekinah before it was too late. On the Damascus road Paul saw its true nature. What is, in the Divine estimation, the very highest possible quality ("if any man thinketh he hath whereof he might glory in the flesh, I more") of legal righteousness? Paul tells us — "dung."

The good senses of righteousness are (1) the righteousness of God *imputed* to him who believes on Christ, in justification (Rom. 3:22; 4:5-8), and *imparted* in regeneration (Gal. 2:20; 1 John 4:15); and, (2) that character which is the "fruit of righteousness" (Rom. 6:17, 18; 8:4). And this righteousness is simply "Christ Jesus, who of God is made unto us . . . righteousness" (1 Cor. 1:30).

Come back now from this necessary *excursus* to Galatians 2:21, the Apostle's third proposition — righteousness, whether imputed or imparted, whether of standing or state, is by faith and *not* by law. If it is not so, then Christ is dead in vain. Are any of our under-the-law brethren ready for *that* alternative?

Second Address (2:15–3:24)

In chapter 3, verse 2, the *fourth* step forward is taken. The Holy Spirit is received by faith, not by the works of the law. Observe, friends, the tremendous *accumulative* force of these successive positions. Each principle, by itself, is enough. If even the Jew must be justified by faith apart from works, that is an end of the matter surely for a poor Gentile. If the law has condemned and executed the sinner who believes, then surely he is not justified by what killed him. If righteousness is by faith and not by law, surely it is folly to seek it by law. So each of these principles spells deliverance. But now there is a fourth principle: The Galatians received the Holy Spirit by simply believing. If, then, God has already sealed them (Eph. 1:13), to what purpose add law-works? (Acts 10:44-48; 11:17, 18; 15:7-11).

Even this does not, however, exhaust the Spirit's reasons why justification is by faith and not by law-works. He takes another position, the *fifth*. Salvation, as we all agree, is under the Abrahamic covenant (Gen. 12:1-4; 15:1-7). Is that a by-faith, or by-law covenant? The question answers itself: Abraham believed God, and it was counted unto him for righteousness (Gal. 3:6-9).

The law was not given till four hundred and thirty years after the call of Abraham—so not only did Abraham not *have* the law, but he was not even *circumcised* (Rom. 4:10).

And now, *sixth*, the Apostle faces the law question directly (3:10-13):

(1) The law cannot justify nor help to justify, for it curses *all* (3:10).

(2) But that curse has been borne by Christ on the tree; and Christ's cross work effected redemption.

Here is the third great word of Galatians. *Justification* and *righteousness* we have looked at—what is *redemption?*

The fundamental idea of redemption is *to acquire by purchase*. The price we know—the awful cost of Calvary. But we shall understand redemption better if we call to mind that three words are translated "redemption": *agorazo,* to buy in the market; *exagorazo,* to *buyout* of the market; and, *lootroo,* to set loose, or free. How wonderful!

Think of our condition; slaves in the market, under the sentence of death. Will anyone buy?

"Perhaps; what is the price of *that* slave?"

"Oh, one price on each; whoever buys must take the slave's place and die."

"Will anyone buy at that price? Will the law redeem? Here is Caiaphas, the high priest. Ho! Caiaphas, will you die for this sheep?"

Second Address (2:15–3:24)

"Certainly not," answers Caiaphas; "sheep must die for me."

"Will no one buy at this awful cost?"

Yes, the Holy Son of God will pay even that price. He, friends, bought us in the market, bought us *out* of the market, set us free. That is redemption.

(3) The law curses, but there are two things the law does not do: it neither adds a new condition to the Abrahamic covenant, nor does it disannul the old condition of simple faith (3:15-17).

And (4) the Apostle answers the inevitable question: Why then the law? (3:19-23). If it does not alter nor in any way affect the Abrahamic covenant, why was it given? His answer is: It was added because of transgressions—and this in three senses:

(a) Sin becomes *transgression* only when there is a law about it (Rom. 5:13). To transgress is to "step over," and there must be something to step over before there can be transgression. Sin of course *existed*, and was inherently evil, before the law, but it had not the character of transgression, nor was it imputed or "put to the account" of the sinner (Rom. 5:13).

(b) The law brought home to the sinner the knowledge of his guilt (Rom. 7:7; 3:20). Coveting, for example, is so "natural" that no one would know it was sinful if the law had not said, "Thou shalt not covet."

(c) The law taught man the deep inherent evil of his nature. What but evil could that nature be which is provoked to sin by a holy, just, and good law? (Rom. 7:8, 9).

That such is the effect of law our own consciousness, our own observation, affirms. Forbid a child to do something which it never thought of doing, and straightway it will long to do it.

You have heard, doubtless, of the Florentine in the middle ages who boasted that he had never been outside of Florence. He was born in Florence, and would live and die in Florence. Hearing this, the reigning duke sent him an imperative order never to go outside the walls of Florence. From that day the man spent his life in longing to go. He would go down to the gates and weep because he must stay within.

The law, friends, is a most necessary ministration to self-deceitful, self-righteous man. It is "holy, just, and good" (Rom. 7:12), and the more spiritual we become, the more we see with awe, and also with delight in so perfect an expression of the holiness of our God, the great "ten words" from Sinai. But we do not seek to be *saved* by it. As Mr. Moody used to say: "The law is a good looking-glass in which to show a child how defiled its face is, but who would think of washing the child's face with the looking-glass?"

Furthermore, the Apostle points out that the law was our pedagogue "unto Christ" (3:24). In

Second Address (2:15–3:24)

the authorized rendering of verse 24 the term "schoolmaster" is misleading. It is a most inadequate rendering of the Greek *paidagogus,* from which we have our English word *pedagogue.* But with us, too, pedagogue means "teacher." The pedagogue in a Greek household was the servant who had charge of the minor children. Over their behaviour, their mental and moral training, he was supreme, having even the authority to administer chastisement. That, then, was one aspect of the law. As the Apostle goes on to say, the Jews under the law, though heirs, differed nothing from servants. As minor children were under the pedagogue, so the Jewish people were under the law: "Now I say, That the heir, as long as he is a child, differeth nothing from a servant, though he be lord of all; but is under tutors and governors until the time appointed of the father. Even so we, when we were children, were in bondage under the elements of the world" (Gal. 4:1-3).

And this, as we shall see in the next address, prepares the way for the Galatians to understand by contrast how their position in grace differs fundamentally from that of the Jew under the law.

At present we close with the emphatic declaration: "But after that faith is come, we are no longer under the pedagogue" (v. 25). Whatever may be our thoughts or our fears, however it may seem to land us in a kind of spiritual anarchy, let us never be afraid to set to our seal that

God is true. What we are under will appear later, if God will; but for better or worse we are no longer under the pedagogue. We may be sure it is for better and not for worse.

Chapter 3

THIRD ADDRESS
(3:25–5:24)

We are to study together at this time the fifth section or division of the Epistle to the Galatians. Surely it will be felt by us to be a most vital and necessary part of this great teaching when we remember that our last study left us without instruction as to the rule of the believer's life.

It is just at this point that modern theology has fallen into the second form of the Galatian heresy. Apparently appalled by the simple word of God, "no longer under the pedagogue," timid Protestantism has indented the gloss: "Not under the law as a *means* of life, but under law as a *rule* of life." It is ingenious and neat, but has the grave demerit of contradicting all that follows.

Section V
The Rule of the Christian Life
(3:25 to 5:24)

Before we look at this, suffer a prefatory word. There is such a thing as mere fleshly exultation in what seems to be liberty not to obey God. That is antinomianism, lawlessness, mere spiritual and moral anarchy. The renewed heart longs unspeakably to do the whole will of God. The inner man delights in the law of God. His agony (Rom. 7:18-24) is that though he delights in the law, he cannot *do* the law:

> *For I know that in me* (that is, in my flesh,) *dwelleth no good thing: for to will is present with me; but how to perform that which is good I find not. For the good that I would I do not: but the evil which I would not, that I do. Now if I do that I would not, it is no more I that do it, but sin that dwelleth in me.*
>
> *I find then a law, that, when I would do good, evil is present with me. For I delight in the law of God after the inward man: But I see another law in my members, warring against the law of my mind, and bringing me into captivity to the law of sin which is in my members. O wretched man that I am! who shall deliver me from the body of this death?*

And, conversely, the true ground of exultation in deliverance from law is that what the law

Third Address (3:25–5:24)

could not do in that it was weak through the flesh (Rom. 8:3) grace perfectly does through the Spirit.

One repels with indignation the imputation of antinomianism—a condition abhorrent alike to God and to the renewed heart. The true antinomians are those who by keeping the believer under the law effectually prevent him from real obedience.

Let us now take these things up in due order. As if anticipating the timorous gloss of modern theology, the Apostle opens this part of the epistle by denying that the believer is under law in any sense: "But after that faith is come, we are no longer under a pedagogue" (3:25). No evasion is possible here. The pedagogue is the law (3:24); faith justifies, but the faith which justifies also ends the rule of the pedagogue. Modern theology says that after justification we *are* under the pedagogue. Here is a clear issue, an absolute contradiction between the Word of God and theology. Which do you side with?

Having laid down the principle that the saint is no more under the law as a rule of life than the sinner was under the law as a *means* of life, the next step is taken—the believer is a son, not a servant; an adult, not a child (3:26–4:7). The words are perfectly plain, and exposition seems almost an impertinence. The thought is that the Jew was under the law because, though a child, he was not a son.

THE EPISTLE TO THE GALATIANS

Sonship in the New Testament is not so much a word of relationship as of position. It is a word, also, of dispensational import. In other words, the Jew under the law was from birth to death a child. He never came to his majority.

In Roman parlance, he never wore the *toga virilis* of an adult. That is the force of chapter 4, verses 1 through 3. Therefore, being a child, not an adult, he was kept under the tutorship and governorship of the law, and differed nothing from a servant. That is precisely the place where modern theology would keep the believer of this dispensation.

But in contrast with the Jew under law, the believer of this dispensation is *born* into sonship: "As many as received Him, to them gave He authority (power) to become the sons of God, even to them that believe on His name: which were born . . . of God" (John 1:12, 13). This is the truth of Galatians 3:26: "For ye are all the sons (R.V.) of God through faith in Christ Jesus."

But this could not be without redemption (4:4-5). In Galatians redemption is twofold: from the *curse* of the law (3:13) and from *under* the law (4:5).

The Old Testament saint had not the Spirit of sonship, because he was a child, not a son; but, because we are sons, we have received the Spirit of sonship, crying in our hearts, "Abba, Father" (4:6). Adoption, again, is a word of position, not of relationship. The word means literally "placing as a son." We are *born* sons, but the Holy

Spirit indwelling the believer gives him the realization, the consciousness of his sonship. The Apostle's conclusion is, "Wherefore thou art no more a servant, but a son" (4:7).

It should be needless to add that all this has in view only the question of the authority of the pedagogue. It is the believer in relation to the *law* which is the question, not the believer in relation to *God*. As regards the law, the believer is a son and not under it; as regards the Father, the believer begins new life as a babe (1 Peter 2:2); and is ever the Father's dear child (Eph. 5:1), and little child (1 John 2:1, etc.); and this is, of course, realized in experience. But positionally he is an adult son, and not under the law. So far the Spirit is mentioned only in relation to sonship, but later we shall find the Apostle showing us that in this mighty fact of an indwelling Spirit in every believer lies the potentiality of an obedient and holy life.

> *The true antinomians are those who by keeping the believer under the law effectually prevent him from real obedience.*

Meantime, he reminds the Galatians that, in putting themselves under law, they have lost, *not* their salvation, indeed, but their *blessing:* "Where is then the blessedness ye spake of? for I bear you record, that, if it had been possible, ye would have plucked out your own eyes, and have given them to me" (4:15). Under grace they were so blessed that they would gladly have given the Apostle their eyes. Where is that blessing now?

The truth is, friends, that an apathetic, dull, inexperienced Christian may get on after a sort under law as a rule of life. Not apprehending that the law is anything more than an ideal, they feel a kind of pious complacency in "consenting unto the law that it is good," and more or less languidly hoping that in the future they may succeed better in keeping it than in the past.

So treated the law is wholly robbed of its terror. Like a sword carefully fastened in its scabbard, the law no longer cuts into the conscience. It is forgotten that the law offers absolutely but two alternatives—exact obedience, always, in all things, or a curse. There is no third voice. "Cursed is *everyone* that *continueth not* in *all things* which are written in the book of the law to do them" (Gal. 3:10). "For whosoever shall keep the whole law, and yet offend in one point, he is guilty of all" (Jam. 2:10).

The law has but one voice: *"What things soever* the law saith, it saith to them who are under the law: that every mouth may be stopped, and all the world may become guilty before God" (Rom. 3:19). The law, in other words, never says: "Try to do better next time." The law, friends, either approves or curses—a fact of which the antinomian legalist seems entirely unaware. Professing to be under the law, his conscience becomes seared as with a hot iron. He stands before the thunders of Sinai unmoved.

But the Apostle would fain bring the whole legal discussion to an end that he may turn to the power which is able to govern the life and produce holiness of character (4:21-31). His final word concerning the law, then, is the revelation of the true spiritual meaning of the domestic history of Abraham.

Hagar is the law. And, it may be remarked in passing, herein is the complete refutation of another gloss of theology—the notion that in all this tremendous discussion Paul is talking only of the ceremonial law. It would suffice in answer to this to ask if the redemption of Christ had reference only to the ceremonial law? For the Apostle speaks but of "the law." But the revelation of the allegory settles forever that evasion: "For these are the two covenants; *the one from the Mount Sinai,* which gendereth to bondage, *which is Agar*" (4:24). Hagar, then, is the *whole* covenant from Sinai. And the conclusion is perfectly explicit: "So then, brethren, we are not children of the bondwoman" (4:31); and therefore "the son of the bondwoman shall not be heir with the son of the freewoman" (4:30).

In other words, law and grace are diverse, contrasting principles, and can no more be mingled than oil and water. Grace is invariably by faith (Gal. 2:21; 3:11-12; Rom. 3:24; 4:4-16; 5:2; 11:6).

The law, let it be repeated, was given for a great and necessary work preparatory to grace.

That is its true place of deathless honor, of holy (if terrible) impressiveness; but it was given neither to make us righteous (Gal. 2:21), nor to rule us, when grace through faith has made us righteous.

We may close for the present with Paul's solemn admonition to legalists, the real antinomians:

> *Desiring to be teachers of the law; understanding neither what they say, nor whereof they affirm. But we know that the law is good, if a man use it lawfully; knowing this, that the law is not made for a righteous man, but for the lawless and disobedient, for the ungodly and for sinners, for unholy and profane, for murderers of fathers and murderers of mothers, for manslayers, for whore-mongers, for them that defile themselves with mankind, for menstealers, for liars, for perjured persons, and if there be any other thing that is contrary to sound doctrine. (1 Tim. 1:7-10)*

Chapter 4

FOURTH ADDRESS
(3:25–5:24 continued)

Let us gather up in a brief word that which was before us yesterday. We saw, first of all, that at verse 25 of chapter 3 the subject changes. Verse 24 ends the section on justification. Justification is shown to be by faith because it is under the Abrahamic covenant, which is a by-faith covenant. Under it Abraham himself was justified—declared righteous and that before circumcision was instituted, and centuries before the law was given. It became necessary, therefore, for the Apostle to show the relation of the law to the Abrahamic covenant. Did it, for example, annul that covenant? Did it add a new condition to that covenant? No, says the Apostle; neither. In a word, the doctrine is that it was added to teach guilty man his absolute need of the grace of the Abrahamic covenant; and, moreover, was a rule of life, a pedagogue, over God's minor children, the Jews. But that was only "unto Christ."

Since, then, justification is by faith, the only question remaining is this: Are we who are the believers of this dispensation, and who are justified by faith, still under the law, the pedagogue, as a rule of life? The Spirit's answer is: "After that faith is come, we are no longer under the pedagogue" (3:25).

As this is the very *crux* of the controversy between the Gospel of God's grace and the Galatianized legalists, who, in much outward and no doubt sincere veneration for the law, insist upon setting it to do work for which it was never made, it may be well for us to turn for a moment to another great passage on this very subject—the sixth chapter of Romans.

In that passage, as in the fifth division of Galatians, the subject before the Spirit's mind is *the rule of the believer's life — not* at all the question of his justification, which has been triumphantly demonstrated to be by faith (Rom. 3:19 to 5:12). The question is, what shall be the manner of life of the justified one? The Apostle puts it in the strongest possible way: "Shall we continue in sin, that grace may abound?" (Rom. 6:1).

And that, friends, is the real question. The curse of sin is gone because of Christ's work; how shall the *dominion* of sin be broken? That is the subject from Romans 6:1 to 8:4. Accordingly, the demonstration follows the order of Galatians: death, resurrection, newness of life.

Fourth Address (3:25–5:24 continued)

But in Romans the discussion is ampler. Into the detail it is not at present our place to go, for we are studying Galatians, not Romans. Let it suffice, therefore, to note that in Romans the Spirit meets the contention that the believer is under the law as a rule of life with an even more emphatic negative than in Galatians.

The question, remember, is never one of evading the will of God, but of getting that will done—a thing the law never did (Heb. 7:18-19). Here is the statement, a statement so concise and emphatic that it can be evaded by no possible device of antinomian legalism: "For sin shall not have dominion over you: for ye are not under the law, but under grace" (Rom. 6:14).

Remember, once more, the matter at issue here is not a means of life, but a *rule* of life; not a way to escape the will of God, but a way to escape the *dominion of sin.* Here, surely, is an end of controversy. If I say I am not under law, and stop there, I am left in spiritual anarchy. If I say I am under the law *and* under grace, I am in the current Galatian heresy which seeks to combine law and grace.

If I say I am not under the law *but* under grace, I am giving a Biblical and Christian testimony.

But enough at this point. I have dwelt thus at length upon it because it is vital to a holy life. In resurrection the believer is not lawless, but is *en nomos Christou* – "in-lawed into Christ" (1 Cor. 9:21).

And now we are ready to turn from the negative to the positive side of the fifth section of Galatians—*the secret of a holy and victorious walk.*

Section V — Continued
The Means of Sanctification in the Christian Life
(3:25 to 5:24)

We shall find the principle and the power of that walk defined in the latter part of the section—Galatians 5:16-24. The *principle* of the walk is briefly stated: "Walk in the Spirit, and ye shall not fulfill the lust of the flesh" (v. 16).

The Spirit is shown in Galatians in a threefold way. First, He is received by the hearing of faith (3:2). When the Galatians believed, they received the Spirit. To what end? The Judaizers made little of the Spirit. Their modern successors make little of Him. Though they talk much of "power" in connection with the Spirit, it is power for service which chiefly occupies them. Of His sovereign rights, of His blessed enabling in the inner life, there is scant apprehension. But it is precisely there that the Biblical emphasis falls.

In Romans, for example, the Spirit is not even mentioned until we have a justified sinner trying to keep the law, utterly defeated in that attempt by the flesh, the "law in his members," and crying out, not for help, but for deliverance (Rom. 7:15-24). Then the Spirit is brought in with oh what marvelous results! "The law of the Spirit of life in Christ Jesus hath *made me free* from

Fourth Address (3:25–5:24 continued)

the law of sin and death" (Rom. 8:2). Not—Oh, hear and heed—not the Apostle's effort under the law, nor even the Spirit's help in that effort; but the might of the indwelling Spirit, breaking the power of indwelling sin.

Then, in Romans, the truth as to the Spirit of sonship is brought in: "For as many as are led by the Spirit of God, they are the sons of God. For ye have not received the spirit of bondage again to fear; but ye have received the Spirit of adoption, whereby we cry, Abba, Father. The Spirit itself beareth witness with our spirit, that we are the children of God: And if children, then heirs; heirs of God, and joint-heirs with Christ; if so be that we suffer with him, that we may be also glorified together" (Rom. 8:14-17).

> *The believer feels the conflict, for it is within him, but he participates only by yielding all to the Spirit. He is not a combatant, but the subject of the conflict.*

In Galatians the order is reversed. First, as we have seen, the Spirit is received by faith; second, the Spirit giving the sons their place (4:4-7); and, third, the Spirit governing the life and delivering from the power of the flesh (5:16-24).

You ask, and necessarily at this point, what is it to walk in the Spirit? The answer is in verse 18: "If ye be led of the Spirit." But how else, friends, may we be led of Him unless by yieldedness to His sway? There is a wonderful sensitiveness in the blessed Spirit's love. He will not act in and over our lives by way of almightiness, forcing us into conformity. That is why "yield" is the great word of Romans chapter 6, where it is expressly said that we are not under the law, but under grace.

The results of walking in the Spirit are twofold—negative and positive. Walking in the Spirit we shall not fulfill the lusts of the flesh. The "flesh" here is the exact equivalent of "sin" in Romans 6:14: "sin shall not have dominion over you."

And the reason is immediately given (5:17). The Spirit and the flesh are contrary, and the Spirit is greater and mightier than the flesh. Deliverance comes, not by self-effort under the law—that is Romans 7—but by the omnipotent Spirit, who Himself is contrary to the flesh. Permit me to detain you here until this vital truth is made clear.

The believer is the subject of a threefold conflict. Until a sinner believes, he is "flesh," "sin," as to his nature. How absolutely he is such is to be learned only from Scripture. No sinner feels the extent of his badness. Living under the stimulus of the Christian ethical ideal now disseminated throughout Christendom; and under the repressive influence of public opinion, formed, roughly speaking, upon that ideal, his heart, "deceitful above all things and desperately wicked," easily persuades him that he is not

Fourth Address (3:25–5:24 continued)

so bad as Scripture asserts. With belief and the new birth comes the new man, the divine nature (2 Peter 1:4).

Instantly there is a conflict, the conflict of the two natures; of the two "I's": Saul of Tarsus and Paul the Apostle, so graphically described in Romans chapter 7. The issue of that conflict is defeat. The new man is "a babe" (1 Peter 2:2) and the flesh is strong in dominion. Moreover, the effort to produce a holy character under the law is foredoomed to failure.

The second phase of conflict of which the believer is the subject is that which is before us in Galatians 5:16-24. But here, and this is the important point, a new antagonist against the flesh is present—the Holy Spirit. It is no longer the two "I's" of Romans 7; it is flesh and Spirit. The believer feels the conflict, for it is within him, but he participates only by yielding all to the Spirit. He is not a combatant, but the subject of the conflict. Austria and Prussia, in the time of Frederick, warred for Silesia. Silesia felt the shock of the conflict, for it was waged upon her soil, but mightier contestants were deciding the issue. So the believer is just heart and soul on the side of the Spirit against the old self, the flesh, but the Spirit wins the victory. The result is inner peace and outward victory over the works of the flesh.

The third conflict is not "against flesh," but "against principalities, against powers, against the world rulers of this darkness, against the spiritual hosts of wickedness in the heavenly" (Eph. 6:12) and is not at present the subject of our study.

The point to hold is that, negatively, the works of the flesh may not be done by the believer who is walking in the Spirit—i.e., is yielded to the Spirit's sway and control.

The works of the flesh are enumerated. It is very searching. Some of these "works" we abhor. We are quite ready to be delivered from adultery, murder, and drunkenness, for example. Are we quite ready to give up variance, emulation, wrath? If we consciously hold to anything contrary to holiness we are not walking in the Spirit. May the Lord make our yieldedness thorough—a root and branch matter!

Then we come to the positive side of the walk in the Spirit:

> There is abroad in the land a most pernicious and misleading phrase—"character building." It is set before us in countless sermons and with most wearisome reiteration that the business of a Christian is to build character. And character building is conceived of after this wise: Character is made up of certain attributes, graces, which may be conceived of as building-stones. Faith lays the foundation, Christ. On Him we build, let us say, honesty, courage, humility, piety, courtesy, etc.—laying stone upon stone. And we are told that character building as a process is carried on by two master masons, Choice

Fourth Address (3:25–5:24 continued)

and Habit. The favorite platitude is, I believe: "The sum of our choices determines character; habit fixes character." Doubtless the mistranslation of 2 Peter 1:5-7 ("Add to your faith virtue, etc.") is responsible for much of this—the true rendering being: "In your faith provide virtue, etc.," as all know. But the legalistic spirit is at the root of it all—even of the mistranslation.

But Scripture conceives of holy character far otherwise as to method and results—far otherwise, and far more vitally:

"Reflecting as a mirror the glory of the Lord, we are changed into the same image from glory to glory as by the Lord the Spirit" (2 Cor. 3:18).

"For it is God which worketh in you both to will and to do of His good pleasure" (Phil. 2:13).

"I live; yet not I, but Christ liveth in me" (Gal. 2:20).

"For to me to live is Christ" (Phil. 1:21).

Note, now, how simply yet how adequately both the quality and the method of the true Christian character is set before us in what is here said upon the affirmative side of the walk in the Spirit (Gal. 5:22-23).

What, first of all, is Christian character? It is love, joy, peace, long-suffering, gentleness, goodness, faith, meekness, temperance. And every one of these graces is an exotic, foreign to the soil of the natural heart. Whence come they? Out of the heart, the nature of Christ. What is Christ, essentially, and apart from His offices and relationships? He is love, joy, peace, long-suffering, gentleness, goodness, faith, meekness, temperance. Christian character, then, is Christ's excellencies reproduced by the Spirit in a renewed life.

Now we ask, what is the method? How, or by whom, are these graces produced in the renewed life? Ah, that is the vital question. For the beatific character is not set forth as an external model to be imitated, but as something which we are to become. We are, somehow, to be love, joy, peace, and the other six lovely graces. What is the method? Can law effect this transformation? Can the law make me love, joy, peace? Hear the Apostle: "Sin, taking occasion by the commandment, wrought in me"—love, joy peace? No. "All manner of concupiscence" (Rom. 7:8).

Precisely there, at the method of the holy and beautiful life, is God's controversy with the antinomian legalists who, seeming to honor His law by putting His dear sons under it as a rule of life, really prevent Him from producing in them the righteousness of the very law they pretend to honor—a righteousness which He can only produce in those who "walk not after the flesh, but after the Spirit" (Rom. 8:4).

But what, finally, is the method? "The fruit of the Spirit is love, joy, peace, long-suffering, gen-

Fourth Address (3:25–5:24 continued)

tleness, goodness, faith, meekness, temperance."

Christian character, then, is not an edifice, but a fruit. And the fruit is the fruit of the Spirit, not of effort, nor of law. In that one "fruit" resides a nine-fold quality, substance, flavor, so to speak. It is vital, aggressive, militant, triumphant. It has in it every element of character which perfect obedience to the law could produce, and beyond law, perfections and graces never contemplated in the law—the very perfections and graces of Christ Himself. One who keeps all the commandments is "an unprofitable servant." Was Christ an unprofitable servant? Were Paul, and Peter, and John, and Barnabas, and Timothy, and Persis, and Phebe, and Priscilla, and Tryphena, and Tryphosa, and the great host of the saintly and of the "quiet in the land," who have walked in the Spirit in holy liberty down to this very day, unprofitable servants?

Chapter 5

FIFTH ADDRESS
(5:25–6:18)

We come now to the sixth and final division of this great epistle, and in it we shall find the outworking in life of the principle of grace as contrasted with the principle of law—of the walk in the Spirit as contrasted with the walk under the law.

The division begins with verse twenty-five of the fifth chapter: "If we live in the Spirit, let us also walk in the Spirit." Legalism would say: "Live in the Spirit by all means, but walk under the law." Not so the Scripture. Life and walk are alike "in the Spirit."

Has it seemed to you, friends, that Paul's great discussions in this epistle have been somewhat theologic, somewhat academic, somewhat doctrinal? Have you been saying: "But how does all this work out—what kind of Christians shall we be in walk and service if we let go the state of nonage, the rule of the pedagogue, and live in the Spirit?" If this question has been in your hearts, then I want to say two things about it.

And *first*, that it partly misconceives the case. For the righteousness of the law *is* fulfilled *in* us (a very different thing from *by* us), who walk not after the flesh but after the Spirit (Rom. 8:4). What we never could do in respect of the law, the Spirit does *in* us.

And *secondly*, the outworking of the new principle is indicated in the very exhortations and instructions before us. Let us look at this beautiful picture of a spiritual, as distinguished from a legal, life.

It begins in that which lies nearest — the brotherhood of believers, and our first concern is to be the ministry of restoration: "Brethren, if a man be overtaken in a fault, ye which are spiritual, restore such an one in the spirit of meekness; considering thyself, lest thou also be tempted" (Gal. 6:1).

What is to be done in case a Christian shall sin? That surely is a test case. And it is the very case the nomolaters, or law-worshippers, would put. "Your grace doctrine," they say, "tends toward looseness of life — toward sin. What resource have you in such a case?"

We answer that first of all the Scripture says that it is not grace but law which is the "strength of sin" (1 Cor. 15:56; Rom. 7:8); and again that we know what the law says about sinners: "The soul that sinneth, it shall die. . . . Moses said that

Fifth Address (5:25–6:18)

such should be stoned." But what does grace say? "Ye which are spiritual, restore such an one in the spirit of meekness."

There is something just under the surface here which is very sweet. The word rendered "restore" is a surgical term, and is used for re-setting a dislocated limb. What happens when a believer sins? Is he cast out of the body? By no means; but he is dislocated as regards service and fellowship. If your arm is dislocated at the shoulder it no longer obeys your will. You may command it to pick up a book, but it hangs, inert, unresponsive. Furthermore, your arm is thoroughly uncomfortable—as we might say, unhappy. Use and blessing are suspended, but *your arm is still a member of your body.*

Now this, we are told, is a very dangerous doctrine. Amazing statement! Because your arm is not lost, therefore you will be utterly careless about mere shoulder dislocations! I have been so foolish as to suppose that those whose limbs have suffered dislocation became exceedingly careful about such risks ever after.

Ah, friends, the renewed heart which, through sin, has suffered the loss of communion with that heart's Beloved; which has learned in darkness the loss of the light and comfort and joy of His fellowship, ever after walks more softly with God.

But for such the spiritual have a ministry so difficult as to test every quality of the fruit of the Spirit. Oh, what love and long-suffering and gentleness and meekness and goodness and faith the ministry of restoration requires! The law has no resource for resetting dislocated members. It is work, indeed, which taxes the utmost resources of grace. For no one is so hard to get on with, no one is so critical, so unreasonable, as a saint out of communion. But, thank God, love can do it, which is a most practical outcome of this walk in the Spirit.

And the next instruction is very like the first: "Bear ye one another's burdens" (verse 2). If you will have law, there is law for you; but you will never find it in the ten commandments—it is "the law of Christ." Truly, we "are not without law to God, but inlawed to Christ" (1 Cor. 9:21). If you want an interpretation of that saying here is one: "Bear ye one another's burdens, and so fulfil the law of Christ." And here is another: "Hereby perceive we the love of God, because He laid down His life for us: and we ought to lay down our lives for the brethren" (1 John 3:16).

Burdens! What a burdened world we live in! Poverty is a great burden. "But whoso hath this world's good, and seeth his brother have need, and shutteth up his tender mercies from him, how dwelleth the love of God in him?" (1 John 3:17). Ah, but he is imprudent, and shiftless, or he would not be poor. Brother, listen: Did it never occur to you that shiftlessness and improvidence are themselves amongst the heaviest of life's burdens? Your brother's poverty is due to shiftlessness, lack of energy, of forethought, say you? Well, then, be thrift and energy and forethought for him.

What a burden *a tarnished name* is! The man is saved, he is your brother, but he brought to Christ a bad record. Every now and again it will block his way, will be brought up against him. Yes; no doubt. Brother mine, let you and me go apart a moment, where all these people cannot hear, while we read: "Some men's sins are open beforehand, going before to judgment; and some men they follow after" (1 Tim. 5:24).

> *There is nothing in the ten commandments to require prisoner Paul to strain his aching eyes to write of grace to the Galatian churches. "The love of Christ constraineth" to that kind of service.*

And there are burdens of *sorrow*—oh, how sympathy lifts them! Yes, it is a burdened world in which we live.

And what shall I, who am under grace, do with my *own* burdens? Bear them myself, if no one comes to my help: "For every man shall bear his own burden" (6:5). I am to remember that, however sorely I am burdened, someone bears a still heavier load, and I am not to go about burdening the burdened with my burden. But if a brother comes cheerily to my side, and if he says, "Brother, let me get underneath your heavy load and lift with you," then I may welcome him, and rejoice that he is fulfilling the law of Christ.

There is a weak and unworthy shifting of our burdens, and of that we will not be guilty; but neither will we churlishly refuse the most Christly help and comfort and cheer of a brother. So there is no conflict here. The second and the third instruction harmonize.

The fourth instruction is the one upon which we who labor in the Word find it difficult to touch: "Let him that is taught in the Word communicate unto him that teacheth in all good things" (6:6).

Bear just here with a word or two. At no point of holy living is the average saint so flatly, wilfully disobedient as just at this point. For example: We are gathered here at a Bible Conference. Unless it is wholly different from other Bible Conferences, the expense of it, and whatever fellowship there may be with teachers, will be participated in by very few. It is so in the churches. Now Scripture speaks, in grace, very plain words about this:

"Even so hath the Lord ordained that they which preach the Gospel should live of the Gospel" (1 Cor. 9:14).

"If we have sown unto you spiritual things, is it a great thing if we shall reap your carnal things?" (1 Cor. 9:11).

Fifth Address (5:25–6:18)

Observe how *personal* this is: "Let *him* that is taught communicate unto *him* that teacheth." In that very personal touch of thoughtfulness, sympathy—in a word of *fellowship*—lies all the grace and sweetness of it. Who wants to have "fellowship" with a collection box? But enough! Just read what follows, and let that suffice. But remember that the Spirit is not speaking here to sinners about their sins, but to saints about their meanness: "Be not deceived; God is not mocked: for whatsoever a man soweth, that shall he also reap."

How vitally true that is! No man, able to fellowship the Gospel, ever yet omitted it and took away a blessing from a teaching meeting. He may have taken away some of that knowledge which puffeth up; but never yet a blessing.

And this brings us to the great law of spiritual husbandry. The two facts—"flesh" and "Spirit"—abide. Every act, every expenditure of thought, strength, or money, is seed sown in one or the other of these soils.

Mr. Moody used to tell of his astonishment when once in a great conservatory in England he saw a gardener take out his sharp knife and cut down a most flourishing branch of a rose bush, leaving only a small shoot to grow. In explanation the gardener told Mr. Moody that it was a grafted rose bush. The shoot cut down was the worthless old stock; it was the other shoot from which the gardener expected roses fit to lay upon his master's table. "Well," said

Mr. Moody, "this is a splendid illustration of Galatians 6:8." (This verse reads: "For he that soweth to his flesh shall of the flesh reap corruption; but he that soweth to the Spirit shall of the Spirit reap life everlasting.")

What follows is more personal, but is most touching: "Ye see with how large letters I have written unto you with mine own hand" (6:11).

The Apostle was, it appears from many considerations, afflicted with ophthalmia, a common disease in the Orient, to the point of almost total blindness. Ordinarily, therefore, he availed himself of the services of an amanuensis, simply adding his superscription. But here, having no scribe at hand, but feeling the urgency of the danger of his dear Galatians, he has written—we cannot know with what of pain and difficulty—with his own hand.

What a gentleman Paul was! He cannot send the letter without a word of apology for the "large letters" his difficult vision compelled him to use! Do you see, friends? How does grace work out, you ask? Well, Paul is not thinking of his "large letters" and the pain and difficulty of his service as illustrating the outworking of grace, but we may. There is nothing in the ten commandments to require prisoner Paul to strain his aching eyes to write of grace to the Galatian churches. "The love of Christ constraineth" to that kind of service.

No, Paul will not glory in himself, but nothing shall hinder his glorying in the cross: "But

Fifth Address (5:25–6:18)

God forbid that I should glory, save in the cross of our Lord Jesus Christ, by whom the world is crucified unto me, and I unto the world" (verse 14). We need not go outside this very epistle to learn why Paul gloried in the cross:

1. Paul gloried in the cross because there the Son of God "gave Himself for our sins, that He might deliver us from this present evil age" (1:4). In that cross Paul saw God Himself take up the whole question of his sins and so deal with his guilt that it no longer existed before the face of heaven. So dealt with his sins that now he could fling out his triumphant challenge to the universe: "Who shall lay anything to the charge of God's elect?" (Rom. 8:33). Is not that something to glory about?

2. Paul gloried in the cross because he had himself died there with Christ: "I am crucified with Christ: nevertheless I live; yet not I, but Christ liveth in me: and the life which I now live in the flesh I live by the faith of the Son of God, who loved me, and gave Himself for me" (2:20). The law in slaying Christ there had slain *him*: "For I through the law am dead to the law, that I might live unto God" (2:19). Henceforth he was become dead to the law. The law having slain him had exhausted its demand. "The law hath dominion over a man as long as he liveth" (Rom. 7:1), but no longer. Now Paul could do what he could never do under the law—he could "live unto God." So he will glory in the cross that set him free.

3. Paul would glory in the cross because there Christ had redeemed him from the *curse* of the law at the awful cost of being made a curse for him: "Christ hath redeemed us from the curse of the law, being made a curse for us: for it is written, Cursed is every one that hangeth on a tree" (3:13). He had been "of the works of the law," and the law had cursed him: "For as many as are of the works of the law are under the curse: for it is written, Cursed is every one that continueth not in all things which are written in the book of the law to do them" (3:10). But Christ had come and lifted that dreadful curse from Paul, that Paul might be redeemed.

4. That cross was at once the manifestation and measure of the personal love of Christ for him, Paul: ". . . the Son of God, who loved *me*, and gave Himself for *me*" (2:20). Here, friends, is something so wonderful that I would we might all enter into it. It is more wonderful, even, than the cloud on Sinai into which Moses entered. It is this: In His death Christ not only saw and loved us *all*, but He saw and loved *each* of us. This is distinctly stated by Isaiah: "When thou shalt make His soul an offering for sin, He shall see His seed . . . He shall see of the travail of His soul, and shall be satisfied" (Isa. 53:10, 11). The death pangs of Christ were the birth pangs of the new creation, each member of which is born separately and redeemed separately. Of that great compensatory vision, each of us may say, He saw *me*, and gave Himself for *me*.

Fifth Address (5:25–6:18)

5. Paul gloried in the cross because by it he was redeemed from "under the law," that he might receive the placing as a son (4:5). The cross did not redeem Paul from the curse of the law only to leave him still under that which not only had righteously cursed him, but must continue righteously to curse "as many as are of the works of the law" (3:10).

6. Paul gloried in the cross because it made possible his mightiest blessing next to deliverance from the curse — the indwelling of the Holy Spirit: "And because ye are sons, God hath sent forth the Spirit of His Son into your hearts, crying, Abba, Father" (4:6). Paul well knew that the holy anointing oil could come only upon atoning blood (Ex. 29:20, 21), and that only because of the cross could he ever have received the Spirit. What a new reason for glorying in the cross!

7. And Paul would glory in the cross, finally, because it made an end of things between him and the world: ". . . the cross of our Lord Jesus Christ, by whom the world is crucified unto me, and I unto the world" (6:14). Ah, friends, here is something very searching. It is one thing to glory in the cross because by it we are become dead to the law — are we as ready to exult in that by the cross we also are become dead to the world, and the world dead to us? Let us remember — and it is most solemn — that it is perfectly possible to glory in the cross in an utterly mistaken and carnal way. Are we willing

to see in the cross only what might gratify self? Do we so degrade and misinterpret the cross as to imagine that Christ redeemed us from the curse of the law, and from the law, only that we might enjoy this present evil age? To Paul the cross stood not only between him and the wrath of God, but between him and this great world-system of ambition, greed, and mere pleasure. Do we glory in this, too?

The Christian Doctrine of the Law

1. Law is in contrast with grace. Under the latter God *bestows* the righteousness which, under law, He *demanded* (Ex. 19:5; John 1:17; Rom. 3:21; 10:3-10; 1 Cor. 1:30).

2. The law is, in itself, holy, just, good, and spiritual (Rom. 7:12-14).

3. Before the law the whole world is guilty, and the law is therefore of necessity a ministry of condemnation, death, and the divine curse (Rom. 3:19; 2 Cor. 3:7-9; Gal. 3:10).

4. Christ bore the curse of the law, and redeemed the believer both from the curse and from the dominion of the law (Gal. 3:13; 4:5-7).

5. Law neither justifies a sinner nor sanctifies a believer (Gal. 2:16; 3:2, 3, 11, 12).

6. The believer is both dead to the law and redeemed from it, so that he is "not under the law, but under grace" (Rom. 6:14; 7:4; Gal. 2:19; 4:4-7; 1 Tim. 1:8, 9).

7. Under the new covenant of grace the principle of obedience to the divine will is inwrought (Heb. 10:16). So far is the life of the believer from the anarchy of self-will that he is "inlawed to Christ" (1 Cor. 9:21), and the new "law of Christ" (Gal. 6:2; 2 John 5) is his delight; while, through the indwell-

ing Spirit, the righteousness of the law is fulfilled in him (Rom. 8:2-4; Gal. 5:16-18). The commandments are used in the distinctively Christian Scriptures as an instruction in righteousness (2 Tim. 3:16; Rom. 13:8-10; Eph. 6:1-3; 1 Cor. 9:8, 9).

GRACE

2 Corinthians 8:9

Like the sheep of the fold, we have all gone astray,
    But One seeketh for you and for me,
Who would fain bring us back to the fold of His love,
    By His grace all-sufficient and free.
O the depth of the riches of infinite grace,
    To be found in the Savior of men!
With His heart of compassion and mercy and love,
    He forgives us again and again.
When His waves and His billows have over us passed,
    And our way is as dark as can be,
Like the Sunshine His promise illumines our path,
    "MY GRACE IS SUFFICIENT FOR THEE."
Can the mind of man fathom the depth of God's grace?
    Can a mortal its fullness e'er know?
Not until he can measure the depth of man's sin,
    With its misery, sorrow, and woe.
Grace reveals to the sinner his sin-burdened heart,
    Grace alone sets the penitent free,
By his faith in the blood of the Crucified One
    Who hath died to redeem you and me.
He hath died but is risen and coming again,
    In the Rapture His children to meet.
May there be in our hands many trophies of grace,
    To lay down at our Lord's pierced feet.

—Gertrude R. Dugan

OTHER BOOKS & BOOKLETS
BY
GRACE GOSPEL PRESS

available through
amazon.com & barnesandnoble.com

10 Principles to Ponder When the Unexpected Happens by Shawn Laughlin

Bad News for Good People and Good News for Bad People: "You Must Be Born Again!" (John 3:1-21) by Dennis M. Rokser

David: A Man after the Heart of God by Theodore H. Epp

Disciplined by Grace by J. F. Strombeck

Don't Ask Jesus into Your Heart: A Biblical Answer to the Question: "What Must I Do to Be Saved?" by Dennis M. Rokser

Faith & Works: A Clarification of James 2:14-26 by Dennis M. Rokser

Freely by His Grace edited by J. B. Hixson, Rick Whitmire, and Roy B. Zuck

Getting the Gospel Wrong by J. B. Hixson

The Gospel by Ron Shea

The Gospel of the Christ by Thomas L. Stegall

Grace: The Glorious Theme by Lewis Sperry Chafer

Holding Fast to Grace by Roy L. Aldrich

I'm Saved! Now What? by Dennis M. Rokser

I'm Saved But Struggling With Sin! Is Victory Available? Romans 6-8 Examined by Dennis M. Rokser

Interpreting 1 John by Dennis M. Rokser

Job: A Man Tried as Gold by Theodore H. Epp

The Judgment Seat of Christ by Samuel L. Hoyt

Let's Preach the Gospel: Do You Recognize the Importance of Preaching the Gospel to Both the Unsaved and the Saved? by Dennis M. Rokser

Must Faith Endure for Salvation to Be Sure? by Thomas L. Stegall

The Need of the Hour: A Call to the Preaching of the Supremacy and Sufficiency of Jesus Christ, Verse-by-Verse, from a Grace Perspective by Dennis M. Rokser

Never Alone: From Abandoned to Adopted in Christ by Becky Jakubek

Planting & Establishing Local Churches by the Book by Dennis M. Rokser

The Powerful Influence of the Christian Woman by Donna Radtke

Promises of God for the Child of God by Dennis M. Rokser

Repentance: The Most Misunderstood Word in the Bible by G. Michael Cocoris

Salvation in Three Time Zones by Dennis M. Rokser

Seven Key Questions about Water Baptism by Dennis M. Rokser

Shall Never Perish Forever by Dennis M. Rokser

Should Christians Fear Outer Darkness? by Dennis M. Rokser

The Strombeck Collection by J. F. Strombeck

A Tale of Two Thieves by Shawn Laughlin

Trophies of God's Grace, Volume 1

Truthspeak: The True Meaning of Five Key Christian Words Distorted through Religious Newspeak by Michael D. Halsey

Where Faith Sees Christ by C. I. Scofield

For other helpful resources from a biblically-based, Christ-honoring, and grace-oriented perspective, please visit us at:

www.gracegospelpress.com